I0803738

Breathing Room

Breathing Room

Beth Gobeil

Hagios Press

Copyright © 2015 Beth Gobeil
Reprinted 2017

All rights reserved. No part of this publication may be reproduced, stored in a retrieval system, or transmitted in any form or by any means without the prior written permission of the publisher or by licensed agreement with Access: The Canadian Copyright Licensing Agency. Exceptions will be made in the case of a reviewer, who may quote brief passages in a review to print in a magazine or newspaper, broadcast on radio or television, or post on the Internet.

A CIP catalogue record for this book is available from Library and Archives Canada.

ISBN: 978-1-926710-34-1

Edited by Paul Wilson
Designed and typeset by Donald Ward
Cover Art: photograph by Camila Carlow, titled "Lungs"
Photographs inside the book: Donovan Gobeil
Cover design by Tania Wolk, Go Giraffe Go Inc.
Set in Minion Pro
Printed and bound in Canada

The publishers gratefully acknowledge the assistance of the Saskatchewan Arts Board, The Canada Council for the Arts, and Creative Saskatchewan in the production of this book.

HAGIOS PRESS
Box 33024 Cathedral PO
Regina, SK, S4T 7X2,
hagiospress@accesscom.ca
www.hagiospress.com

Contents

Claiming the Sky

Donovan 10
Diagnosis 11
The Knowing 12
Flawed 13
Omens 14
New Normal 15
Playing House 16
Dreaming My Son's Funeral 17
Bitter 18
Shadows 19
Acoustics 20
Advice 21
Uninvited 22
A Delicate Balance 23
A Wish 24
Untethered 25
Terry Fox Award 26
Driving Lessons 27
Our House 28
Tracing the Route 29
Thin 33
Over the Salad Bar 34
My Son Needs a Lung Transplant 35
Getting Ready for Winter 36
A Prayer 37
Claiming the Sky 38

Every Little Thing

Every Little Thing 40
The Quilt 46

And Now

Letter 62
Transplant Tree 63
At Five 64
Unlearn 65
Reading the Fine Print 66
Fear of Rejection 67
Unpacking 68
Another Inch 69
Circle 70
Brother 71
The First Time I Saw You 72
Renovations 73
Now 74
Hope Lives 75
Breathing Room 76

Afterword 77

Acknowledgements 79

For Donovan Michael Laurier Gobeil
and for his lung donor
who passed the baton to him.
The journey is yours, son.

And

In loving memory of my brother-in-law
Colin Paul Gobeil
1963–1988.

But those who trust in the Lord *will find new strength.*
They will soar high on wings like eagles.
They will run and not grow weary.
They will walk and not faint.

— Isaiah 40:31

Claiming the Sky

Donovan

The night he was born,
an orange globe of moon
hung low in the late August sky.

I cradled him
as he struggled for first breath,
eyes squeezed tight.

We called him Donovan,
didn't know we had christened him
Dark Warrior
or that he was fighting
even then,
his hands balled
into small fists
as the enemy lurked
inside.

Diagnosis

In some dark crevice
there was an intuition, a certainty
I tried to ignore
even as I breathed the antiseptic air,
pulled my baby's small arm
from his blue fleece sleeper
before the lab tech took him away.

On some level I was sure
as they gathered,
white-coated backs to me
and spoke in hushed tones.

Before the surreal drive home
the phone's insistent ring,
the doctor's compassionate words
I played over and over,
as if to convince myself of what
I already knew.

The Knowing

You are stoic
when they tell us:

Cystic Fibrosis

The disease that stole your brother
at twenty-five
will lay claim to the baby
you hold sleeping
in your arms.

You who can repair anything:
kids' toys, our old wagon,
dilapidated back steps
you will fix this, too.

That cloudless June day
at the water park, he is three,
steps on the edge of his blue beach towel
trips and skins his knee;
falls just out of your arm's reach.

That night, your tears soak my shoulder
your chest heaves with the knowing,
you cannot fix this —

he will always be
just beyond your reach.

Flawed

two genes, one
from each of us

both
flawed

equally
responsible

I absolve
you

and shoulder
this

alone

defective
mutant

my silent
flagellation

Omens

Because I eschewed insects,
swept ladybugs and grasshoppers
from my house.

Few snakes crossed my path
or cows for that matter,
mourning cloaks and luna moths did not enter
my windows.

I didn't take in stray dogs
afraid that they would bite,
and when birds flew over
my head was always covered.

I should have kept both eyes open
for four leaf clovers,
worn summer dresses inside out

and studied spider webs
more carefully
to find my initials.

New Normal

We count weeks without illness
instead of new baby teeth

stack pill bottles like they
are building blocks

clap his back to make him cough
no time to play pat-a-cake

make countless trips to hospitals and specialists
instead of visits to great aunts or old friends

cheer for higher lung function scores
like they are straight-A report cards

redefine *normal*
when each moment

is singular
each breath, a signal.

Playing House

The two of you kneeling on the playroom floor
in front the pink dollhouse your father and I constructed one Christmas.
In this game Barbie has *sick-sick five roses*
has to have needles and take medicine. She coughs and coughs.
A tiny spoon travels from a chubby hand to her practiced smile.
She is turned upside down while her back is clapped:
Cough it up, cough it up. Spit it out.

The mother cries.

The father goes to work.

Dreaming my Son's Funeral

The playground near our home
turned cemetery,
his sandy grave.

The gathered mourners leave,
I stand and remember him
clear and bright as a summer day
his laughter carried on the wind
through the swings and carefree trees
of his childhood.

I cannot leave him here
do not know how
to say good-bye.

I pick up sand,
watch the grains
slip slowly through
my fingers.

Awake to the sound
of my sobbing
rush to gather him in my arms,
need to feel the warmth of his breath
on my cheek,
steady thump of his heartbeat.

Bitter

We hear new terms:

bronchiectasis, pneumothorax

words weighty as dinosaurs,
this medical jargon, a language
I never set out to learn.

Ciprofloxacin, Ceftazidime, Tobramycin

Names of a dozen antibiotics
how to read x-rays
what the white streaks mean,
interpret numbers on
pulmonary function tests.

The mother tongue of this illness
leaves a bitter taste in my mouth
like the small green apples
I ate as a child, an ache in my gut,
deep and dull as that.

Shadows

In the x-ray
I see feathers, clouds
the kind that streak a summer sky.

Infection, says the doctor
scarring; permanent
and irreversible

raindrops, oval shadows,
tears.

Acoustics

The discordant music of illness
fills our home;
strains of laboured breathing echo
at the top of the stairs,
end of the hall.

Coughing punctuates sentences
sometimes staccato,
sometimes the sputtering of an engine
refusing to turn over.

Nebulized medications
purr and hiss
inhale, exhale
a cloud of mist heard
over morning radio
and nightly news.

The hollow *thump* of chest percussions,
familiar bass rhythm
of hand hitting ribs,
and lungs being cleared.

Feeding tube pump
a nocturnal lullaby,
grind and whirr
grind and whirr

till we don't even hear it
at all.

Advice
(from a CF mom)

When the lab loses the test result
and your kid has to be poked again and again,

lose yourself in a John Grisham novel,
emerging only to devour dark chocolate.

When you've played *doctor-go-round*
for five endless days,

advise your friend on her marriage
like *you* are some kind of expert.

When your child's cough keeps you up all night
even with the third antibiotic,

cut your hair, rearrange furniture
or sew colourful living room curtains.

When you miss the middle kid's
kindergarten graduation,

buy her a new bike
and lie to your mother-in-law.

When your sick child asks, at the age of thirteen
if he should write his will, *just in case*

pull on your tattered Nikes, find a lonely stretch
of road and run.

Uninvited

Like an uninvited guest
illness moves in, makes itself at home
refuses to leave.

It unpacks with a sense
of belonging,
and has a gift for creating chaos.

We tiptoe around at first
and give it what it needs,
but like a spoiled child
it just demands more;
keeps an exhausting schedule,
stays up late
and rises far too early.

We don't do anything
without checking first,
always hoping
to catch it in a good mood,

while it holds us here
like hostages —

we worry this will end
in bloodshed.

A Delicate Balance

Our bodies are suspended, star-fished
on the water's surface,
through mask's distortion
we search for a flash of fin, dart of colour
turquoise, yellow, blood red
a dream-like blur.

Look, look this one!
your finger follows Butterfly and Angelfish
we exchange smiles
with sky-wide eyes,
we want to get closer
to feel the crust of colours.

Alive and dying,
everything is connected
below the water's thin skin

Look we are told
but do not touch.

A Wish

Donovan takes pictures,
viewfinder pressed against his eye
he zooms in, sharpens the image
reads the light meter
snaps the shutter release,
and a moment is frozen in time.

Flocks of Cedar Waxwings
descend on our backyard Mountain Ash,
moonlight spills onto a northern lake at dusk
a spider creeps across its delicate web,
dewdrops like diamonds
in morning sun.

I wish I could do that
for him:

capture his life,
soften
all the edges.

Untethered

When Donovan watches his agile brother,
I wonder if his memory takes the shape of his lithe body
to that time when it was him who loped with ease.

Does his mouth, still thirsty, drink the wind
at the finish line, hands-on-knees
throat dust-dry and burning,
and when he cheers
does he recall that praise for him?

He takes close-ups of his brother,
with head bowed low,
the medal's weight and victor's smile;

at night when he lays sleeping,
with each breath's push and pull
the steady tide of his chest's rise and fall,
does he run untethered?

Terry Fox Award

On a shelf in Donovan's room,
half-hidden by some CDs
instructions for installing his car stereo,
postcard from a friend's vacation,
a blue velvet box:
inside, a gold medal embossed with the image
of Terry Fox as he hop-stepped the highway.

The night they gave it to him
friends packed city council chambers,
spilled into the foyer to catch a glimpse.

He sat stiffly in his new black suit,
fingers smoothing the crease marks
on his folded acceptance speech,
shielding his eyes
from the flash of cameras
as they read letter after letter
extolling his courage.

He, not wanting any of this:
the long receiving line,
the hugs and handshakes

he tucks that blue velvet box away
the moment he gets home.

Driving Lessons

Donovan teaches me to drive;
he tells me with certainty I brake
too far ahead of the stop sign,
accelerate too quickly,
that I don't shoulder check before a lane change,
even the radio, set to the wrong station
is changed with a stab of his finger.

I suck in air between clenched teeth
grip the wheel till knuckles whiten,
remind this kid I diapered
I have been driving for thirty years,
thirty years!
My indignation occupies
the seat between us.

Exactly, he says. *Far too long to remember*
the rules of the road.

On his face a smug smile,
newly dried ink on his license
qualifying him to dish out driving tips
like potato chips.

Today my son teaches me how to drive,
tomorrow, he'll be a set of tail-lights
on a road to some new place,
self-assurance telling him
that anything is possible.

Our House

Signs of it everywhere now,
in the basket of mail between ads for pizza,
power bill and a prescription to be filled:
a blue and white inhaler.

Can't miss it in the cupboard
which once held salt and pepper,
peanut butter and jam for morning toast,
a row of digestive enzyme bottles
six capsules with each meal,
treatments multiplying like odd socks.

Tubes snake from cardboard boxes
stacks of gauze pads, a sharps container,
door that barely closes,
towels moved to bathroom shelves.

IV pole, as out of place
among the cast-off clothes
and book-strewn night stand
as a Christmas tree in July.

Visitors avert their eyes,
and don't ask.

Tracing the Route

1.

A soft knock on our bedroom door,
the half-light of dawn
silhouettes
the fear in his eyes,
in his hand a crumpled tissue
crimson stained

his half-spoken words:
I coughed blood.

And in the space
of startled seconds
I am reeling
through the moonless night
beneath the weight of words,
beyond this time, this breath
to a place where
no one is bleeding.

2.

I won't look at the monitor
numbers falling,
level of oxygen fed into
my son's starving lungs,
his fingernails dusky, hands cool,

in the cardboard basin
a splatter of blood with each cough;
controlled panic in the doctor's voice
as she suggests another hospital.

I need to do something:
feed him ice chips,
fold a cold cloth for his head
breathe for him,
then me.

3.

The ambulance is cramped, the ride bumpy
Donovan sleeps beneath a white blanket.

I think of our motorhome,
summer trips with him asleep
on the fold-down table,
as we travelled at night,
I held the map
my finger tracing the route.

I have no map for this road,
a trip we didn't pack for,
a destination that holds no anticipation,
the paramedic's chatter interrupted by radio static
his pen and clipboard charts my son's vitals;

I stare at the night sky, the rush of stars
search for the moon, still as Donovan's sleeping form,
something steady and familiar to follow.

4.

I hurry down the hall and pause,
startled by laughter
coming from room 332,
the Donovan Gobeil suite
we've dubbed it
having been here so often.

I open the last door on the right
his friends sprawl around the room
on chairs, his bed, the the window sill,
they crouch in corners hugging their knees.

They regale him with stories,
party on the weekend, *so lame,*
you didn't miss a thing!
The new chemistry teacher, who is *so harsh,*
piles of English assignments, and who slow danced
with whom at the Halloween Howl,
as if he were with them all along.

They've grown used to the IV pump,
oxygen tubing, nurse who comes in to hand him
a small paper cup, check his central line,
pulse oximeter, blood pressure
are not startled by his rasping cough,
the way he winces with pain,
and hold his chest.

They help him make selections from
the three-day menu
knowing he eats so little,
kid about what is offered:
mystery meat, cream of lump soup
they bring him zesty taco chips and root beer.

Staff overlook visiting hours,
announcements on the intercom
do not apply,
room checks, ignored.
These faces, this laughter, vital as any drug;
they walk the long hallway,
hurry off to part-time jobs at A&W,
collect homework to drop off
feel better Donny, love you bud.

5.

In a box on Donovan's bed tray
are spread
a thousand tiny pieces.

We work the puzzle methodically
sort pieces by colour, start with edges
create a frame, fill in bit-by-bit.

Colours confuse, details shift
after a dozen attempts, *a-ha!*
A piece is snapped into place.

Day by day hands arrive to help:
a nurse solves a maple tree, visitors
construct a row of gabled houses
and a winter landscape emerges,
children dress a snowman
with a pebbled smile and a woolen hat.

What has been fractured
will take time to rebuild. For now,
we will settle for the simple act of seeing —
something here wishes to be whole.

Thin

The line I walk,
is each day, a little
thinner,
and higher
from the ground.

In my arms,
the weight
of children, illness, husband.

I can't hold them all,
am afraid
to look down,
I stare into the blur
of distance

and take small steps,
imagine
an outstretched hand.

Over the Salad Bar

In the hospital cafeteria
I recognize my son's specialist.

He tells me he is giving the usual cocktail
of antibiotics, rest and chest physio,
should turn him around in a few days,
he says, scrutinizing lettuce to add
to the styrofoam bowl in his hand.

But we need to discuss a lung transplant.
His tone is casual as he reaches with the silver tongs
for a crisp piece of celery and alfalfa sprouts.

I'll send a letter to Edmonton,
he spoons on bacon bits and chick peas
my secretary's on strike, things are a mess
you have no idea, he confides, *it might take a while*
he sprinkles dry noodles on top of his salad.

Didn't expect we'd be at this point so soon,
he says ladling thick white dressing on the heaping bowl,
I'm kinda surprised to tell you the truth
with a look of disgust he picks and discards
a leaf of lettuce browning at the edges,
shakes his head and turns to leave.

My son needs a lung transplant.

Stunned, I stare past the plastic guard,
at the coin carrots and vinegared beans in porcelain jars,
who are as stupefied as me.

My Son Needs a Lung Transplant

The hospital walls heave and billow
with the effort of each breath
in a stifling hallway crowded with carts
I rush past the vacant faces of patients,
doctors and nurses with charts.

I run from the respiratory floor
down the stairs piled precariously
on top of each other,
how do I navigate this?

Through the corridors, at last
outside where dark clouds
traverse a troubled sky,
a slowly shrinking sun.

An ambulance screams
and the river slowly
floods it banks.

Getting Ready for Winter

Doctors want to open my boy's chest
like the hood of a car they say,
replace his diseased lungs with a new pair.
If only it were that simple,
straight-forward as tuning up the old Chev:

top off fluids, inspect brakes and belts
check for cracks and leaks
install new snow tires,
and hope it will take us
through one more winter.

The doctor listens to Donovan's rapid breathing,
his cough like a sputtering engine,
he inspects enlarged fingertips, bluish nail-beds,
holds x-rays of his chest up to the light.

He wonders how much longer
he can mend him,
ready him for the rough road,
the hard season ahead.

A Prayer

(for Donovan)

If God can find time
(between painting sunsets, charting tides
and conducting constellations),
I'd like you to go to your graduation,
if it's okay with Him.

For you to wear the new black suit
that waits in plastic film in your closet
pants hemmed two inches,
shiny shoes from Sears.

I want you to walk across the stage,
shake the principal's hand
grasp that diploma,
I want you to smile for a picture
posed under the arch of flowers
to put between those of your sisters
on top of the piano.

Even with war in Iraq and famine in Africa,
I'd like you to go to the dance
to hold that slender girl, her hair up in curls
the two of you swaying.

I know about the hole in the ozone,
the constant threat of nuclear disaster
and the crystal meth epidemic;

but I want it for you
this one night.

Claiming the Sky

On a fishing trip
that summer at Besnard Lake,
his first eagle.

Hand shading eyes from noonday sun
spellbound, he follows its graceful flight
a cross of wings and body,
dance of swoop and glide.

I dream him free
his wings outstretched,

a spirit that rises above the
quiet water of the crystalline lake
beyond the canopy of tall trees
and claims the sky.

Every Little Thing

Every Little Thing

1.

All summer
there was a knowing
that hung in the heavy air around us.
In the hospital we tried to ignore it as we lit a sparkler
for Donovan's birthday cake, his twentieth;
no breath for candles.
Friends with guitars croon
Don't worry 'bout a thing,
'cause every little thing gonna be alright.

2.

We speed to Saskatoon hospital
in the back seat Donovan's breath
comes in quick gasps,
I turn up the dial on his oxygen tank;
he rolls the window down to feel
air rush over his face.
I read from a novel; words he can focus on,
words that don't make the journey
from the page to my conscious mind.

3.

Baptism

In respiratory distress
Donovan is unable to fall asleep,
and says God spoke to him.
Our pastor arrives,
water is poured from a paper coffee cup
over our son's head in the ICU,
while he fights for each breath.

4.

I want to take away his pain,
which seems endless
then, after a light rain,
my husband sees a vivid triple rainbow
maybe a promise,
that our son will live?
Oh me, of little faith.

5.

Wrapped in gauzy layers of sedation
Donovan struggles to free himself,
slow and meticulous he scratches pen on paper:

throat really dry
wet my mouth
I can't spit

what was wrong?
they find bleeding?
what day?
what time?
a.m. or p.m.?
Katie, Amy & Stephen
do they know?

6.

He is weak and so, so tired
but cannot sleep.
I sing the lullabies of his childhood
stay awake, don't rest your head
don't lay down, upon your bed

Anything to slow his rapid breathing,
the pulse that pounds in orange
numbers on the screen above his head.

7.

Don't speak his name
a nurse warns,
Don't hold his hands
or touch his face,
it causes distress.
Don't let on
that you are here at all.

8.

The weekend passes with tears,
prayers and hall-walking.
I try to force food into my body, try to sleep.
I cannot think of anything but my
sick, sick boy,
breathing from a ventilator
fevered, restless.
We come and go
from the ICU
surrendering moments,
hours to God,
hardly speaking to each other.

9.

In the ICU waiting room
I crumple like the tissue in my hand
Enough I tell myself *enough now.*
I grab the black remote
flick from channel to channel,
try to lose myself in the monotony of reality shows,
the unraveling of someone else's life.

10.

Each day my son grows weaker,
a seed of doubt takes root in my heart
and grows a slow and choking vine.

I wander the halls
bracing for the unthinkable.

I look out a window and the sky
closes in, fills a hole within me.

11.

Through the window in the ICU
I watch them tether Donovan's hands to the bed rails
a precaution, afraid in sedated confusion
he will dislodge a line,
this is for your safety, they tell him.

Out the kitchen window, a spring day
I watched him with his dad,
heads bent over the engine of his first car
gift from Uncle Roger, an aging Caravelle
rust etching the wheel wells, freckling the hood
The Batmobile Donovan dubbed it,
lips curving in sly smile

wiping greasy hands on a rag he tucked
in the back pocket of his jeans.

They spoke in a dialect foreign to me
their low voices rumbling through the open window
something about filters, hoses and timing
how to change the oil, check the tires.
I watched them walk back and forth to the garage,
the clink of wrenches filling in silences
saw them toss each other tools,
listen to the start and stopping of the engine.

Side by side they worked until the light faded
at last slammed the hood, came in and scrubbed
black grime from their fingernails
peeled off dirty t-shirts, still talking
fuses, cooling and spark plugs over re-heated supper,
kidding about *that car* and gas prices, then —

the brief tether of his dad's long arms around his bony frame,
how safe he was in that moment,
before they both headed off to bed.

12.

We meet with doctors,
their voices hushed, faces grave
I don't want to look at them
or hear their words:

Your son's condition is critical.
He needs lungs now

and donors are rare.

13.

The decision is made
in a whirlwind —

Donovan will be air-lifted to Edmonton.

We throw clothes into bags
and drive as if in a dream.
I stare out the window
and think of our son asleep
somewhere above the clouds.

14.

Donovan is listed for transplant.

And our wait begins
with the ancient faith
that what is needed
will somehow,
against the odds,
soon appear.

The Quilt

1.

I sit while I wait for word
a torn quilt spread on my lap
a seam that opens wide.

My hands needing something to do,
a needle in my fingers, the point pierces
the orange and brown fabric,
thread pulls the frayed edges of flowers
together stitch by tiny stitch, this,
the one thing I can mend.

2.

I hear the click of a key in the back door
hurried footsteps descend the stairs,
a look on my husband's face I've not seen before
what is he trying to say?
His arms on my shoulders,
I cannot hear this news
I will never be ready for it.

3.

It is as if I am watching
myself from across the room.

I hear this woman
as if from a distance, her voice
a loud and strangled cry
No, no, he can't die!
I don't want him to die!

I observe her
stumble to the bathroom,
feel the dread that clenches
at her stomach. My body jolts
as she retches. My body goes cold
and someone wraps her in a quilt,
someone holds her.

4.

They speak of life-support
a heart/lung bypass machine
a last-ditch effort to save my boy.

5.

In the small room
our family and friends gather,
a tissue box passes hand–to-hand,
so little is left to say.
I stare unseeing
at the gold and green patterned carpet.

My husband walks in, phone in his hand
kneels in front of me, begins to speak slow words
as if to make himself believe
and make me hear this:

They have lungs

6.

Sudden and surprising as the *pop* of a cork
joy fizzes, it foams and overflows,
soaking everyone in sudden celebration.

New lungs from a young male donor, they say
they are bright pink, un-sick, un-CF lungs.

7.

In the waiting room for hours
we talk, pace and wait; eyes on the slow sweep
of the clock as it marks the hours
since they took Donovan that morning,
through doors that yawn open and closed,
the static drone of announcements
the call for doctors:
code blue, code blue.

8.

After seven hours, the doctor
is there in green scrubs
his eyes smiling at us
under a cartoon - print surgical cap
tells us he is all through,
the new lungs are inside our son —
I try to thank him, but my words are tangled
somewhere within me,
and all I can do is hug.
We form a circle of arms,
on this day, there is only love.

9.

We are finally permitted to see our son,
the rise and fall, rise and fall of his chest,
normal breathing…a miracle.
I have never witnessed such silent beauty
so very slow and quiet,
no whirr of a loud respirator forcing oxygen
into reluctant and dying lung tissue
just a soft whisper of breath
his nailbeds —
the most lovely shade of pink.

10.

First off, everyone gets a hug!
No wimpy noodle arms
or 3-pats-on-the-back man hugs,
but a big tight bear hug
with little red cartoon hearts
floating all around
because (as Lloyd Robertson would say)
that's the kind of day it's been. . . .

11.

The doctor says we will need to be patient
with Donovan's slow awakening:
toe-wriggling, shoulder-scrunching,
one-eyebrow raising, my least favourite
his slow eye-ball rolling
then later, two eyes open,
both looking and blinking with interest,
just not at us —
there's something there on the ceiling
that really holds his attention and I'm a little jealous,
but am told hallucinations take precedent
over the living after such trauma.

They say to hang in there;
when all the narcotics are flushed out,
we'll get our Donovan back.

12.

Still, I am on constant red-alert
having walked the mine-field of this illness
battle-weary I call into the ICU,
am put off for "procedures."
What procedure? What is going wrong? Is he ok?
Questions tumble through my fatigued mind
so inwardly jangled I conjure enemies,
I should be there to shield my son.

13.

Talk to us, son, can you hear us?
do you know you have new lungs?

I have used lungs

There's your dad, Donovan, can you say, " Hello Dad?"

I can say hello myself, mom.

I love you, son

I love you too.

14.

They take off your oxygen tubing today
too much oxygen in your blood,
really, *too much oxygen?*
Are those new lungs bragging?

What happened to my dexterity? you ask a doctor.
Wow, a four-syllable word on day three post-surgery.

He replies,
I think your noggin is doing just fine!

15.

We heard your donor was a young man,
just a few years older than you

it isn't him I conjure, this day
the fourth after your surgery

don't ponder possibilities
of how he lost his life

it's you my thoughts
return to.

But somewhere today a mother
is at church,

family, friends,
autumn trees around an open grave

while we are here
still in all-out celebration.

16.

Katie winds tape around the handle
on the suction tube, her brother's
hands are so weak
not knowing where to find it
he has trouble latching on.

She remembers her little brother
when they were skinny–legged
and sun-freckled,
running around the backyard blue spruce
around the trampoline, her voice
bouncing: *Donny Donny Doodlebug*

She winds tape on this handle,
both of them looking now
for something
to hold onto.

17.

Donovan didn't sleep a wink last night,
so this is a valley day.
We pray today is his last
in the 24-hour marathon of the ICU.

He is in a drug- induced fog
of mental confusion and anxiety
and I feel that double-edged sword
as my son orientates himself to time and place.
I tape a note to his bed, a constant reminder,
Donovan, you are in Edmonton, you are safe.
I show him the timeline of his journey,
the path we took, and the way forward.

I'm to bring a mirror to the hospital
so Donovan can see his shark-bite incision
also his iPod; time to get back in touch
with the world he abandoned,
to sleep and recovery.

18.

His white blood count running high — and we don't know why.
Legs swelling, it's worse tonight,
why won't it go down?
His new lungs sound a little crackly.
Could it be infection? Blood sugar
readings are all over the map.
Donovan needed blood yesterday,
puzzling his doctors. Should they be looking
for sources of internal bleeding?
Always, more questions,
of course, nothing is ever obvious.

19.

Katie, Amy and Stephen join us for the weekend,
the whole family together in one room;
I want to keep them within reach forever,
but I'll settle for the time we have together now.

A stroll down Whyte Avenue
in the beautiful autumn weather with golden leaves
falling gently and crunching underfoot,
one day in the not-too-far future
Donovan will walk with us.

20.

Twenty-eight staples,
armpit to armpit, spaced a half-inch apart
holding together the clamshell incision.
we prefer *sharkbite;*
more exciting and dangerous.

At the beach this summer
Donovan will have a massive scar,
and a perilous story
to impress all the girls.

21.

They say miracles don't happen anymore,
not since water was turned into wine,
or an ocean squall was stilled with words.

They say prayers are heard
only by the cupped ear of a full moon,
don't waste your breath.

But when they show us photos of Donovan`s old lungs
beaten up, misshaped and discoloured,
then a photo of his new lungs
beautiful, pink and firm inside his open chest

I am transfixed;
what once was, and what now is —
the evidence of things unseen,
the substance of that
which was prayed into being.

22.

Donovan takes the first voyage out of his room.
He stands with a huge padded apparatus,
adjustable arm benches, handles to grip
a harness underneath to hold him up.
His steps are small and painstakingly slow,
he calls it *the zombie walker.*
I follow behind with his wheelchair
down the hall, up the other side,
his legs trembling when he makes it
back to bed.

23.

While Donovan lays in bed,
his sisters wash his hair.
A complicated system of tray
and plastic garbage bag funnels,
they try hard not to spill on the sheets,
their hands scrub his scalp,
pour fresh water
from a blue jug.

They held their brother's hands,
held their breath for him,
and cried.
Now they wash his hair,
a ceremony, a celebration
with the shampoo that smells of a spring rain,
they rinse and comb and blow-dry
until their brother's brown hair gleams.

24.

(Post-transplant Life Expectancy Statistics; U.S. Scientific Registry of Transplant Recipients)

One year:
Eighty three point six percent

Three years
Sixty six to seventy percent

Five years:
Fifty three percent

Ten years
Twenty eight point four percent

25.

Don't think about your donor
the transplant coordinator says.

Take those thoughts
fold them away,
like the ugly sweater
your grandmother knit

the one you wear only
when she comes for Thanksgiving dinner.

Put those thoughts in the bottom drawer
shut it tight,
and forget.

26.

I watch Donovan in the physio gym,
day by day more fiercely determined
to get his body back,
strengthen his Bambi-on-ice legs.
His muscles are wasted from weeks in bed,
he pumps the barbell
though his arm wobbles and sweat stings his eyes.

27.

One hundred and twenty eight steps
spread over sixteen flights, the hospital stairs.
By-passing the elevator
Donovan scurries up all of them
in pace with his athletic brother
then he overtake his parents,
and keeps one flight ahead.

At the top, flushed and grinning,
he strikes a casual pose; says,
What took you so long?

28.

This weekend ours will be the house
with the "Happy Homecoming" festivities.

How many times will Donovan tolerate my arms
around him before, *Mom, will you lay off?*

My Christmas present this year
is two working, breathing
pink squishy lungs,
all wrapped up in the bony ribs
of my twenty year old boy.

29.

Falling snow leaves a field of diamonds
glinting in the moonlight.
A kitchen candle flickers,
I can hear the cat padding down the hall.
Stephen is strumming his guitar downstairs,
dodging homework.

I glance at the clock counting the hours till I'll hear the car,
the crunch of tires in our driveway, and my heart will be filled
as I see Donovan's lanky figure toting a suitcase
cross the threshold of home.

30.

I pull the mended quilt around my shoulders
and feel the smooth seam, the repair
hidden from all but the most discerning eye,
thread blending with fabric
joining patch to patch,
the camouflaged craftsmanship.

Running armpit to armpit,
your healing incision, the surgeons careful stitches;
your scar, they say, will become silver-white
and fade away.

What heals, joins us
together.
Over time, we are mended,
and made strong again.

And Now

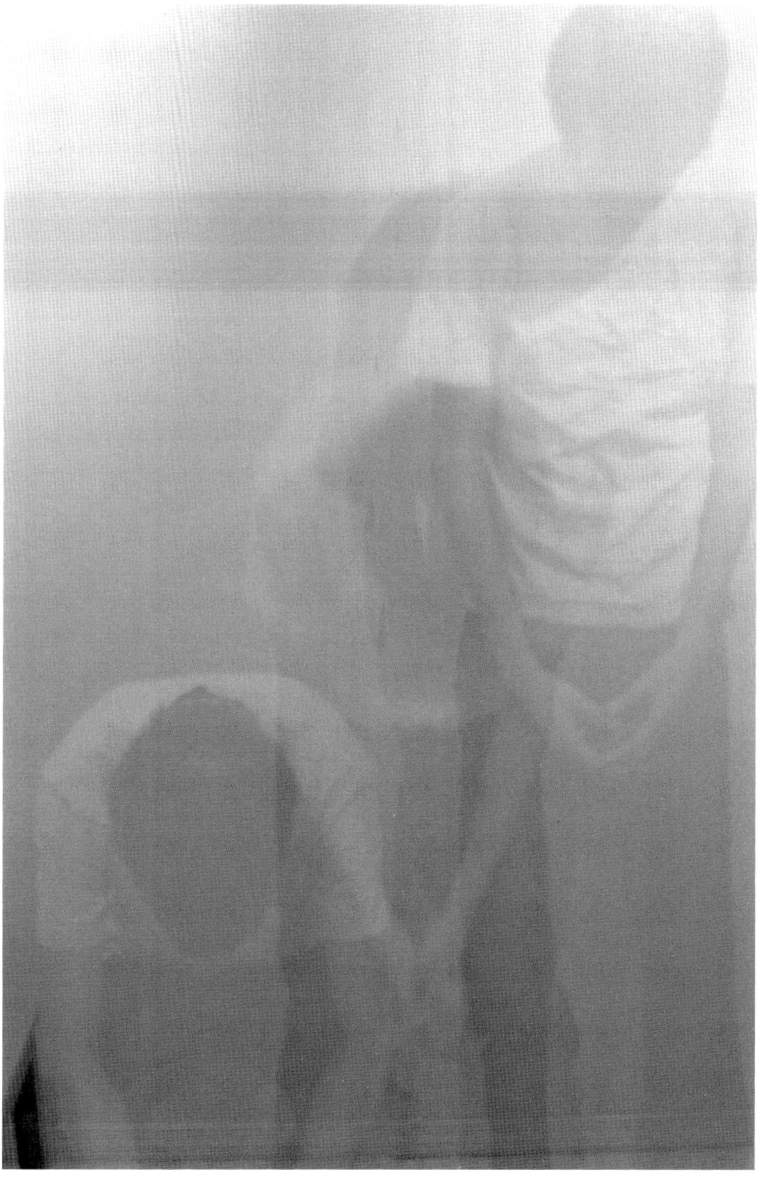

Letter
(To Donovan's donor family)

He came in from a run
slammed the door, sat down to remove his shoes
and socks, which he draped on the back
of a dining room chair.

I start to tell him
take those stinky socks —
when it bubbles up in me
like a geyser,
stinging my eyes
leaving me speechless.

I want to take this moment,
and a thousand more just like it,
and send them to you:

My lanky son, his wind-reddened face,
a smile playing at the corners of his mouth,
his sweaty socks
like first place ribbons,
draped on the back of a dining room chair.

Transplant Tree
(for the lung donor)

In a corner of the yard, we plant a Silver Maple
in memory of Donovan's lung donor,
a sapling, barely five feet tall, only a few scrawny branches.
We stake it to an iron rod for support,
fill in the hole, and tamp down peat moss at its base.
We research when to fertilize, consult neighbours and the internet,
haul pails from the backyard faucet,
work the soil and weed around
the tree's thin trunk .

In winter, we look out the window at a skeleton
stripped of leaves, skinny branches like gnarled fingers
protruding at awkward angles, and question its chances
surviving blizzards and forty below, but come spring,
sure as a promise kept, there are greening buds,
and new branches stretching sunward;
a faint glimmer of silver as light touches
the back of the first unfurling leaf.

We circle the tree and discuss what to prune,
we do what we can, which is really so little,
and watch in wonder as width and height
are gained with each passing year.

It takes two hands now to measure the girth
of the once stick-like trunk, the tree's canopy
welcomes perching sparrows and chickadees;
it no longer depends on us for water, or much of anything,
its roots wandering far and deep, an anchor in all seasons.

At Five

I remember you at five,
the small celebration, the battered two wheeler,
same one your sisters learned on,
buckling the helmet snug under your chin
you're ready, you can do it

your father and I running beside you on the lawn,
a hand on the back of the white vinyl seat,
sisters cheering along, wibble-wobble of the wheels,
gathering speed, one small push,
steady, steady

and down you'd go.

The trauma, the tears, dusting you off,
convincing you back again and again,
your small legs pumping pedals,
overwrought as I sensed just the right moment
to let go.

How to Unlearn

For months you talk of it, prepare me
search the web for jobs, tell your friends
you are leaving home, moving
on to Saskatoon, to your sister's spare room.

Plans as nebulous and airy as the skies
over Candle Lake where you spent the summer.
You worked, but really it was one long party,
wasn't it? Get the campers to sleep,
sneak off to the staff cabin,
stay up all night, drink
the cool air, play guitar.

Home again. August's undoing.
Loads of sand-filled laundry, a cough rough as gravel
that lasts through September, a setback sends us
to doctors, CT scans, diagnosis,
an enemy so familiar.

Some things never change: IV pole
in your bedroom, pill bottles stacked, a tower
on shelves in your new home
where you unfold sweaters,
towels, sheets, your new bold self
all neatly into the life you're creating.

There is silence in the place you leave behind
dust balls, posters, tattered magazines
a man-sized space where the boy once lived.
I redecorate, bed-spread, pillows, pain
of a phantom limb, severed, I still feel you
here, expect you in every room,
call you for meals, then wonder
how a mother is supposed to unlearn.

Reading the Fine Print

1.

This comes with no ironclad warrantee,
in fine print at the bottom of the page.

No ninety-day money-back guarantee,
not even an exchange offered

in case of defective merchandise.
There is nowhere to return the broken pieces.

2.

We don't know what might happen
in another minute, an hour, much less tomorrow.

We don't ponder plans for a week from now
or flip through calendar pages, pencil in hand.

There is no one to bribe for more time,
we can't buy our son a future, at any price.

Fear of Rejection

The transplant clinic hands us a thick binder,
how to manage life with new lungs
the importance of blood
pressure, pulse and lung capacity
and how to record the numbers each day.

They tell us not to worry,
that almost everyone
faces at least one bout
of rejection.
Small reassurance.

And I recall the sting
when the boy I liked
didn't call back,
the job I wanted
but didn't get,
the poems I sent out
that were rejected.

How small those losses
when held up against this:
the suffocating loss
of a body
that would turn away
its very breath.

Unpacking

In this Saskatoon rental house
three eager guys sort a confusion of cords;
x-box, stereo, computer,
flat-screen TV.

My son clothes naked hangers
points a skinny finger
where to place bed, dresser, desk;
his room after all, he's waited twenty-one years
to be Master and Lord of the Manor.

Stock the fridge with milk, eggs
casseroles frozen in plastic containers,
assortment of fruit, nourishment
likely to live and die in the crisper
passed over for pizza,
Wednesday wings at the Longbranch.

We discuss bank accounts, bus schedules,
where to pay the power bill,
minor annoyances
in his independent life.

Remember to call, I want to say,
wear your heavy coat
lock the doors at night.
I'll miss you.

Have fun, is all I manage.

On silent streets
we take home empty boxes,
brimming with words
I couldn't unpack.

Another Inch

Saturday tag-along with your retro-queen sister,
weekend job at the Sally Anne, first dibs on the drop-off bin;
old Stones and Beatle's LPs, T-shirt stamped *Wild Child*,
you re-invent cool.

You test the bulbs of chipped ceramic lamps,
shelve dog eared magazines,
pillows musty from storage
when an old man stumbles in,
matted hair on an unshaven face,
the dark hollows of his cheeks.

Can I help you find something? you ask.

He doesn't speak, but points to his lace-less shoes,
blackened tips of frost-bitten toes poking through,
snow clinging in clumps on his torn pant legs,
you search shelves of second-hand pairs.

You find something serviceable,
and at the till refuse his coins.

No, it's ok. you tell him

both of you living
on a ledge.

Circle

You hold your sister's newborn son,
baby Elijah's fingers, his infinitesimal toes
the velvet of round cheeks.

How grateful I am that you lived to meet him
Donovan, to see this circle complete:
an unbroken family tree,
the perfection of this new bud.

Brother

A friend loves at all times, and a brother is born for adversity. . . .
— Proverbs 17:17

You grew up in waiting rooms,
your childhood, a season spent between
your brother's appointments
and hospital admissions.

You were five years old, if that
and to my astonishment, you read:
keep out, dark room
a sign in the x-ray department.

Trundled to specialists,
you made yourself at home
nesting amid your brother's IV and oxygen lines,
absorbed in video games, movies in the hospital playroom,
consumed uneaten ice cream and cookies
on Donovan's tray when we forgot your dinner.

We carried you sleeping down the elevator
through corridors to the parking lot,
long after visiting hours were over.
We left you for days with relatives and friends,
waiting for your voice on the phone,
your silence touching my own,
uncertain
of the air around you
and if it was safe, finally, to exhale.

The First Time I Saw You

We were in front of the doors to the hospital chapel,
each of us led there by the same sense of desperation
that haunted so many faces in that place.

Mothers of transplant children,
you said you would pray
for me, and I of course, told you the same.
It was your second time around, a year-long wait
for your daughter who had developed rejection,
and I was a rookie, my son, a new recipient,
fighting a fungal infection.

We were parents of kids on the same team, both rooting like mad
for our side, bound in friendship, as if we had any power at all over
the unseen opponent who was constantly one move ahead of us.

I've never told you how hard it was
when Donovan was discharged and we came home.
How I felt I'd abandoned you there, had somehow
betrayed you both, as I reveled in my son's slow
rise to health.

Or how I still feel each thirtieth of June, the day that marks
your daughter's passing. The memory of the first time I saw you, of
two mothers adrift in a sea of unknowns, clinging to each other,
searching for something hopeful to say.

Renovations

The old reno, you say, inspecting the attic,
they took out load-bearing walls.
Years later, and record snow one winter
too much for the weakened roof,
the ceiling sags and threatens to fall.

How much like us, this old roof
the weight of decades on our shoulders
things both said and left unsaid
the inward groan and heave
shifting to carry the load,
knees bending beneath the heaviness.

But you won't let it fall, the house or us;
you climb the ladder with wood and nails, saw
and hammer, work long days, late nights, reinforcing,
patching, you make it strong and straight again.

Now

Nineteen seventy eight, Mr. Comesky's English class,
your cousin in the next desk introduces us in the noisy hallway
a spring day between classes.

You skipped trig to sit with me on the grass by the river,
then called me later, *Laurier from school,*
like I would know, say, ten other guys by that name.

Let me feel the lightness of the gold band,
the naiveté that slipped it on your slender finger;
add the early years, lean as your long arms,
and mine trembling with the weight of our first baby;
recall three houses, a few cars, homework, shiftwork,
your brother's funeral, our fathers, losses like these,
and smaller ones we never speak of.

Now, turn off the light at the far end of the garage
burning late into the night, come in
and hang up your saw-dust sprinkled jacket,
take off your work boots, leather peeling from the steel toes,
come sit with me, let it always be like this.

Hope Lives
(for Donovan & Carla, 2012)

Hope lives for things as annoyingly ordinary
as remembering to check the gas guage
on the way to work. It lives, laughing and chopping,
tasting from the spoons you offer each other. It is there
in your long arms, tender around her small frame
as she washes the dishes.

It joins you on the sofa,
your voices blending like soft music,
heard down the hall as you weave plans
into the night. Hope whispers goodnight,
when she leaves,
and in the morning, listens
for the sureness of her return.

Breathing Room

There is something light now, and easy in the air you breathe.
There is a job, a paycheck and texting with friends
and the roar of your longboard as you sweep
down the drive and carve a corner,
smooth as talk over dinner, your voice assured
as you gesture, fork in hand and claim
you've shaved minutes from your 5K.

There are backyard fires now,
conversations spiraling up to star-sparked skies,
your long outrageous stories and favorite verses of old songs,
tunes you pluck from memory;
there are dances and dates, weekends away.

There is something fluid in the way you move
in and out of your car and your plans,
where there is so much room for you to breathe,
where there is room for all of us.

Afterword

Donovan Gobeil was born on August 26, 1988, a long-awaited brother to big sisters Katie and Amy. He was diagnosed with Cystic Fibrosis (CF) in November of that year, just as we were losing his uncle, Colin Gobeil, to the same disease. Colin died of CF at age 25, awaiting donor lungs.

With a routine of medication and therapy, Donovan was able to enjoy quite a normal childhood, taking part in school activities, soccer, swimming, and playing with his friends. When he was five years old, he became a big brother when Stephen joined the family, a role Donovan very much enjoyed.

As he approached his teen years, Donovan's health began a slow downward spiral, despite aggressive treatment. His lung function declined, and by his last year of high school, hospital stays to fight infection had become routine. Plans for post-secondary education after graduation were put on hold. A double lung transplant became a distinct possibility, somewhere in the unspecified future.

On a Sunday afternoon, August 31, 2008, my husband Laurier and I drove Donovan from our home in Prince Albert, Saskatchewan, to Royal University Hospital in Saskatoon for what we thought would be a short hospital stay to treat a tenacious lung infection. We had no idea then that we wouldn't see home again for nearly six months. After the usual protocol of treatment failed, Donovan was air-lifted from Saskatoon to University of Alberta Hospital in Edmonton, on September 8, 2008, and from there continued a terrifying decline. Donor lungs arrived on September 13, 2008 when our son had literally hours to live.

Things have changed dramatically for Donovan in the years that have passed since he received a second chance at life. He no longer has to endure the hours of chest physiotherapy, nebulized medications, tube feeds, exhaustion, and breathlessness that were a hallmark of his pre-transplant life.

After recovering at home for nearly a year, Donovan worked at various jobs, and then decided to pursue his dream of post-secondary education. He is currently a student of Saskatchewan Polytechnic pursuing a diploma in Addictions Counseling.

As part of his recovery from the surgery, Donovan began working out physically, very much enjoying the new ease with which he could move and breathe. He began a running program and set a goal to participate in the 2012 Canadian Transplant Games held in Calgary, where he received three gold medals in running and cycling events. In September 2014, he ran a local charity race in Prince Albert, completing a 10 km race in just over 51 minutes. He has also run several half marathons.

Most notably, Donovan met the girl of his dreams, Carla Olsen, and on July 6, 2013, a beautiful, rainy summer afternoon, they exchanged vows of marriage at Christopher Lake, Saskatchewan. Donovan and Carla reside in Prince Albert.

I began to write poems about Donovan's and our family's journey with Cystic Fibrosis as part of a creative writing class when Donovan was about sixteen years old. I found this process to be cathartic and as I began to share these poems with him, Donovan said he felt they honoured his journey, as an honest portrayal of life with this chronic disease. As Donovan laid in the ICU prior to his lung transplant, desperately ill, he asked me, "Will you keep telling my story?"

When Donovan was air-lifted to Edmonton prior to his transplant, I began to blog about the events of each day as a way to keep in touch with many family members and friends who were supporting us during this time. The blog can be found at www.donovanstransplantjourney.blogspot.com. It details his transplant and recovery. This blog eventually became poems for the middle section of this collection.

As a family, we are very grateful for the excellent medical care Donovan received from the time he was diagnosed as a baby, and the care he receives to this day. Thank you to: Dr. M. Jurgens, Dr. Ramji, Dr. Bulat, and Dr. Lambos, the wonderful nurses of the paediatric ward at Victoria Hospital, Prince Albert, and to both the paediatric and adult Cystic Fibrosis clinics at Royal University Hospital, Saskatoon. We are also indebted to the wonderful team at University of Alberta Hospital for their excellent care, especially Dr. Ghorpade who performed Donovan's lung transplant, the transplant clinic doctors and staff, and the rehab unit.

We are also thankful to my dear friend Verla Chatsis, who took us in one dark night in Edmonton, and housed us for nearly six months; and also to the Poetker and Hagel families who cared for Donovan's brother Stephen in our absence on short notice.

Acknowledgements

Thank you, Donovan, for gifting me with the privilege of writing this story. It has been an honour paralleled only to the joy of being your mom.

Thank you to Laurier, my husband and partner on this journey for the last three and a half decades, for your faith in me, for your love and encouragement.

Thank you to my children, Katie, Amy, Donovan, and Stephen, who listened patiently and endlessly (and sometimes willingly), to my poems and gave me space and time to write.

Thank you to my mom, Pearl Bernard, and my mother-in-law, Laurentie Gobeil, and to both the Gobeil family and Bernard family members, too numerous to name, for your love, support, and prayers for Donovan as we have walked the journey of Cystic Fibrosis and transplant together.

To my Prince Albert Alliance Church family, to Laurie Domoslai and staff of Wee Care Preschool, and to the community of Prince Albert, including many wonderful friends, thank you for your support in prayer and many acts of kindness from the time Donovan was born to this day. You have kept me breathing!

Thank you to the Children's Wish Foundation of Canada that made Donovan's dream of snorkeling the Great Barrier Reef a reality.

Thank you to my cousin, mentor, friend, and fine poet Lynda Monahan. I would not have written this story without your undying support and encouragement. Lynda, you gave me my voice and told me I had the courage to be a poet, and I am forever indebted to you. Thank you also to the members of Sans Nom poetry group for your support as this manuscript came together. Thank you also to Bruce Rice for his support of this book.

Thank you to Paul Wilson for his keen eye as editor, and to Hagios Press for believing in this project.

The poems "The Knowing" "Renovations," "Now" are for my husband, Laurier Gobeil. "Playing House" is for my daughters, Katie Drader and Amy Gobeil. "A Wish" was written about our family trip to the Great Barrier Reef, Australia, a wish for Donovan that was granted by the Children's Wish Foundation. "The First Time I Saw You" is dedicated to Connie Roy, in memory of her daughter Kristen Roy. "Brother" is dedicated to my son, Stephen Gobeil.

Donovan and Beth Gobeil

Beth Gobeil has published her poetry in *Transition* magazine and in the anthology *Skating in the Exit Light*. Her work has been read both provincially and nationally several times on CBC Radio's *Sound X-Change* program. She has studied creative writing at Saskatchewan Polytechnic (formerly SIAST), and attended Sage Hill Writing Experience under the tutelage of poet Priscilla Uppal.

She lives with her husband Laurier in Prince Albert, Saskatchewan, where she teaches preschool. They are parents to four children, and grandparents to two amazing grandchildren.

The author's royalties from this book will be donated to Cystic Fibrosis Canada and The Canadian Transplant Association.

Cystic Fibrosis (CF) is the most common fatal genetic disease affecting Canadian children and young adults today. Persistent and ongoing infection in the lungs causing destruction of lung tissue and loss of lung function eventually cause death in those afflicted. There is no cure; however, advances in CF research and improved success with lung transplants for end-stage disease has resulted in increased life expectancy, from childhood to adult years. For more information see http://www.cysticfibrosis.ca.

There are more than 4,500 people waiting for organ transplants in Canada today. Too many people die on organ transplant wait lists. A single donor can save up to eight lives. If you want to be an organ donor, let your family know your wishes and register with your province. See organ-donation-works.org for more information.